HANDS-ON HISTORY!
VIKING WORLD

LEARN ABOUT THE LEGENDARY NORSE RAIDERS,
WITH 15 STEP-BY-STEP PROJECTS AND MORE THAN
350 EXCITING PICTURES   **PHILIP STEELE**
CONSULTANT: LESLIE WEBSTER, BRITISH MUSEUM

ARMADILLO

This edition is published by Armadillo,
an imprint of Anness Publishing Ltd, Blaby Road,
Wigston, Leicestershire LE18 4SE; info@anness.com

www.annesspublishing.com

If you like the images in this book and would like to investigate
using them for publishing, promotions or advertising, please
visit www.practicalpictures.com for more information.

Publisher: Joanna Lorenz
Managing Editor, Children's Books: Sue Grabham
Senior Editor: Nicole Pearson
Editor: Louisa Somerville
Designer: Simon Borrough
Illustration: Stuart Carter and Julian Baker
Special Photography: John Freeman
Stylist: Thomasina Smith
Anness Publishing would like to thank the following
   children for appearing in this book: Hazel Askew,
   Christopher Aurokium, Anthony Bainbridge,
   Christopher Brown, Sarah Bone, Jessica Casteneda,
   Eleanor Grimshaw, Mohsin Laher, Victoria Lebedeva,
   Artem Lissovets, Rebecca Miah and Arkan Udoh

PICTURE CREDITS
(b=bottom, t=top, m=middle, l=left, r=right)
The Ancient Art and Architecture Collection Ltd: 3, 4ml, 9tr,
9mr, 10t, 27tr, 32tl, 46tl, 49tr, 50mr, 59ml; Arnamagnæan
Institute, Denmark: 54tl, 55tl; The Bridgeman Art Library:
14mr, 15tl, 17bl, 27bl, 44b, 45tr, 45ml, 53ml, 57bl; The
British Museum: 8tr, 29tr, 46ml; C M Dixon: 13tl, 13ml, 14tr,
16ml, 16br, 17tr, 18tl, 19br, 22ml, 25tr, 27tl, 30mr, 44tr,
47tr, 48mr, 53tr, 57tl, 58ml; E T Archive: 20ml, 24bl, 47tl,
51tr, 56bl; Mary Evans Picture Library: 41tr; Werner Forman
Archive: 17tl, 21ml, 25tl, 34mr, 40mr, 42tl, 45tl, 48ml, 49ml;
Michael Holford: 10m, 16tr, 32–3tr, 36tl, 37tl, 57tr, title page;
Robert Harding: 20tr, 22tr, 23m, 25bl, 27bm, 30tl, 37tl, 38l,
39t, 55ml, 60b; G. Hildebrand 60tl; National Museum of
Copenhagen: 42tr, 61bl; National Museum of Ireland: 59tr;
Pierpont Morgan Library/Art Source, New York: 5r;
Riksantikvaren, Norway: 35ml; Mick Sharp: 10b, 11tr, 13mr,
17br, 18b, 45br, 47ml; Brian Shuel: 61tr; Statens Historik
Museum, Stockholm: 3, 14tr, 26tl, 33ml, 34ml, 40tl, 51m;
University of Oslo: 8mr, 12tr, 23tl, 29tm, 34tr, 35tr, 61br;
Yale University Press: 41m; York University Trust: 2, 11bl,
19bl, 21m, 23tr, 24tr, 25mr, 26b, 28tr, 28m, 29bl, 30ml, 30ml,
31tr, 32m, 35m, 42ml, 43m, 46mr, 49mt, 49m, 53tl, 58tl,
59tl; Zefa Pictures: 12b.

Manufacturer: Anness Publishing Ltd, Blaby Road, Wigston,
Leicestershire LE18 4SE, England
For Product Tracking go to:
www.annesspublishing.com/tracking
Batch: 0878-21488-1127

CONTENTS

The Coming of the Vikings

THE YEAR IS AD795. Imagine you are an Irish monk, gathering herbs to make medicines. Walking along the river bank you hear the sound of creaking oars and curses in a strange language. Through the reeds you see a long wooden ship slipping upstream. It has a prow carved like a dragon. Inside it are fierce-looking men – battle-scarred warriors, armed with swords and axes. Incidents like this happened time after time around the coasts of Europe in the years that followed. In the West, these invaders were called Northmen, Norsemen or Danes. In the East, they were known as Rus or Varangians. They have gone down in history as Vikings. This name comes from a word in the Old Norse language meaning 'sea raiding'. Who were they? The Vikings were Scandinavians from the lands known today as Denmark, Norway and Sweden. Archaeologists have found their farms and houses, the goods they traded, the treasure they stole and their fine wooden ships.

BATTLE ART
The Vikings were skilled artists, as well as fierce warriors. This Danish battle axe is made of iron inlaid with silver and decorated with swirling patterns.

INTO THE PAST
Archaeologists have excavated Viking towns and found ships, weapons and hoards of treasure. This excavation is in York, in northern England.

SEAFARERS
The outline of the Viking ship, with its high prow and square sail, became widely feared. This carving is from the Swedish island of Gotland.

TIMELINE AD750-875

The Vikings were descended from German tribes who moved northwards into Scandinavia over 2,000 years ago. They were restless, energetic people. By the 780s, they were raiding other lands. Soon they were exploring, settling and trading far from home, from North America to Baghdad. By 1100 the Vikings had become Christian and their lands had become more like the other countries in western Europe.

Viking sword

750 Trade opens up between northern Europe and the East. Trading routes are established.

Small trading and manufacturing towns flourish, such as Ribe in Denmark, Paviken on Gotland and Helgo in Sweden.

treasure hoard

789 Vikings raid southern England.

793 Vikings raid Lindisfarne, an island off the north-east coast of England.

massacre at Lindisfarne

795 Vikings raid Scotland and Ireland.

AD750   AD775   AD80(

THE VIKING HOMELANDS

The Vikings came from Scandinavia. This map shows some of the most important Viking sites. Most of these were in present-day Denmark, southern Sweden and along Norway's coastal fjords.

INVASION FLEET

This painting shows Vikings invading England in 866. They went on to defeat and murder Edmund, King of the East Angles. Much of our knowledge of the Vikings comes from accounts written by their enemies. Many of these, such as this one about the life of St Edmund, were written later.

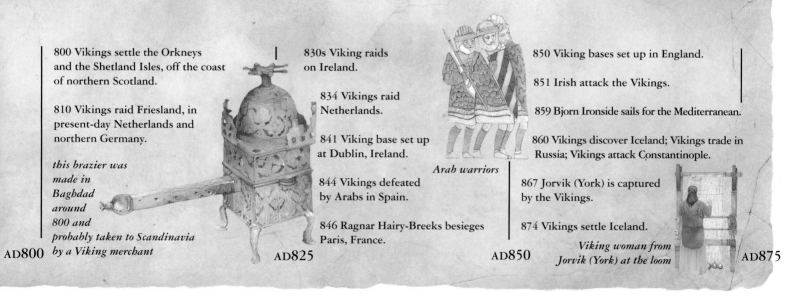

800 Vikings settle the Orkneys and the Shetland Isles, off the coast of northern Scotland.

810 Vikings raid Friesland, in present-day Netherlands and northern Germany.

this brazier was made in Baghdad around 800 and probably taken to Scandinavia by a Viking merchant

830s Viking raids on Ireland.

834 Vikings raid Netherlands.

841 Viking base set up at Dublin, Ireland.

844 Vikings defeated by Arabs in Spain.

846 Ragnar Hairy-Breeks besieges Paris, France.

Arab warriors

850 Viking bases set up in England.

851 Irish attack the Vikings.

859 Bjorn Ironside sails for the Mediterranean.

860 Vikings discover Iceland; Vikings trade in Russia; Vikings attack Constantinople.

867 Jorvik (York) is captured by the Vikings.

874 Vikings settle Iceland.

Viking woman from Jorvik (York) at the loom

AD800   AD825   AD850   AD875

The Viking World

T̲HE VIKINGS took to the sea in search of wealth, fortune and better land for farming. At that time, Denmark was mostly rough heath or woodland. The other Viking homelands of Norway and Sweden were harsh landscapes, with mountains and dense forests, which were difficult to farm.

From the 780s onwards, bands of Vikings launched savage attacks on England, Scotland, Ireland and Wales. They later settled in large areas of the British Isles, including the Orkneys, Shetlands and the Isle of Man. Viking raiders also attacked settlements along the coasts and rivers of Germany, the Netherlands and France. The area they settled in France became known as Normandy, meaning 'land of the Northmen'.

Viking warriors sailed as far as Spain, where they clashed with the Arabs who then ruled it. They also travelled west across the Atlantic Ocean, settling in Iceland, Greenland and even North America.

Viking traders founded states in the Ukraine and Russia and sailed down the rivers of eastern Europe. They hired themselves out as the emperor's bodyguards in the city they called Miklagard – also known as Constantinople (modern Istanbul).

By the 1100s, the descendants of the Vikings lived in powerful Christian kingdoms. The wild days of piracy were over.

N

L'Anse aux Meadows

CANADA

NEWFOUNDLAND (VINLAND)

TIMELINE AD875-1000

carved prow

Viking longship

proclamation of Althing

878 Alfred (whom the Victorians called The Great) of Wessex defeats the Vikings.

885 Viking army attacks Paris.

886 Danelaw treaty in England.

900 Harald Finehair becomes first king of a united Norway.

910 Anglo-Saxon king, Edward the Elder, recaptures large areas of England from the Danes.

911 French give Normandy to the Vikings under King Rollo (Hrolf).

930 One of many meetings of the Iceland Althing. The settlement of Iceland is largely completed.

937 At the Battle of Brunanburh, Athelstan of Wessex defeats an alliance of Danes, Scots and Welsh.

940 Edmund of Wessex makes peace with Olaf of Jorvik.

AD875   AD900   AD925   AD950

GREENLAND

Greenland Sea

Norwegian Sea

Thingvellir
ICELAND

Brattahlid

NORWAY

SWEDEN

HEBRIDES

Kaupang

Birka

North Atlantic Ocean

SCOTLAND

Lindisfarne
priory is
burned

DENMARK

Ribe

Dublin

WALES

York
(Jorvik)

Hedeby

IRELAND

ENGLAND

FRANCE

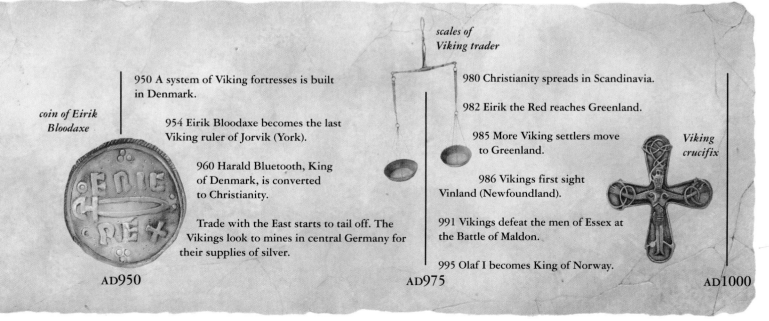

scales of
Viking trader

coin of Eirik
Bloodaxe

950 A system of Viking fortresses is built in Denmark.

954 Eirik Bloodaxe becomes the last Viking ruler of Jorvik (York).

960 Harald Bluetooth, King of Denmark, is converted to Christianity.

Trade with the East starts to tail off. The Vikings look to mines in central Germany for their supplies of silver.

980 Christianity spreads in Scandinavia.

982 Eirik the Red reaches Greenland.

985 More Viking settlers move to Greenland.

986 Vikings first sight Vinland (Newfoundland).

991 Vikings defeat the men of Essex at the Battle of Maldon.

995 Olaf I becomes King of Norway.

Viking
crucifix

AD950

AD975

AD1000

Viking Heroes

THE VIKINGS greatly admired bravery and a spirit of adventure. The names and nicknames of their heroes, who were explorers, ruthless pirates and brave warriors, have gone down in history. Two of the most famous were Ragnar Hairy-Breeks, who terrorized the city of Paris in 846, and a red-bearded Norwegian, called Eirik the Red, who named and settled Greenland in 985.

The Vikings we know most about were powerful kings. Harald Hardradi (meaning stern in counsel) saw his brother, King Olaf of Norway, killed in battle. He then fled to Russia and went on to join the emperor's bodyguard in Constantinople. After quarrelling with the Empress Zoë, he returned to Russia before becoming ruler of Norway.

BLOODAXE
This coin is from Eirik Bloodaxe's reign. He was the son of Norway's first king and ruled Jorvik (York).

Viking women could be just as tough and stubborn as their men. They were well respected, too. Archaeologists found two women buried in a splendid ship at Oseberg in Norway. One was a queen, the other her servant. They were buried with beautiful treasures.

MEMORIAL IN STONE
This memorial was raised at Jelling in Denmark by King Harald Bluetooth. An inscription on it says that King Harald 'won all of Denmark and Norway and made all the Danes Christians'.

FROM WARRIOR TO SAINT
Olaf Tryggvasön was Harald Finehair's grandson. He seized the throne of Norway in 995. King Olaf became a Christian and was made a saint after his death in 1000.

TIMELINE AD1000-1100

1000 Iceland becomes Christian.

1002 Leif Eiriksson reaches Vinland, (Newfoundland).

1014 Irish defeat Vikings at Clontarf.

1016 Svein Forkbeard, King of England, is succeeded by Cnut.

1017 King Cnut rules Denmark.

Anglo-Saxon brooch in Scandinavian style

1028 King Olaf II of Norway is overthrown in civil war.

1030 King Olaf II dies in battle at Stiklestad. He is later made a saint.

King Cnut comes to the throne in Norway.

1035 King Cnut dies. The Anglo-Saxons rule all England.

1047 Harald Hardradi is made King of Norway.

King Olaf II

AD1000 *Viking fighting Native American in Newfoundland, North America*

AD1010

AD1020

AD1030

AD1040

AD1050

THE NORMANS

Hrolf, or Rollo, was a Viking chief. In 911 he and his followers were granted part of northern France by the French king. The region became known as Normandy, and the Normans went on to conquer Britain and parts of Italy.

THE WISE RULER

Cnut was the son of Svein Forkbeard, King of Denmark. He led extremely savage raids on England, becoming king in 1016. As a king, he proved to be kinder and wiser than he had been as a warrior. By 1018 he was King of Denmark and by 1030 he had become King of Norway as well. He died at Shaftesbury in 1035.

LEIF THE LUCKY

Leif the Lucky was Eirik the Red's son. He sailed even further west than his famous father. In about 1000 he reached Canada, sailing to a land he named Vinland. This was probably Newfoundland. Other Vikings, including Leif's brother Thorwald, tried to settle these North American lands, but with little success.

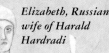

Elizabeth, Russian wife of Harald Hardradi

1050 Oslo founded by Harald Hardradi.

1053 The Norman empire begins in southern Italy.

1066 Harald Hardradi invades England. He is defeated by Harold I at the Battle of Stamford Bridge. An exhausted Harold I is in turn defeated by William of Normandy at the Battle of Hastings.

Norwegian footsoldier with axe

1070 The English pay Danegeld (a ransom) to persuade the Viking raiders to leave them alone.

1080 Cnut IV becomes King of Denmark.

1084 The Normans sack (raid) Rome.

1086 Cnut IV is assassinated.

1087 William of Normandy dies.

1098 King Magnus III of Norway asserts his authority over the Orkneys, the Hebrides and the Isle of Man. Although these were Viking settlements, there was dissent in these places.

1100 End of Viking era.

AD1050　　　AD1060　　　AD1070　　　AD1080　　　AD1090　　　AD1100

9

Viking Society

MOST VIKINGS WERE FREEMEN, or *karls*, who owned some land and a farm, and went to sea for raids and adventures. Other karls were merchants, ship builders or craft workers. The free Vikings used *thralls*, or slaves, as workers and servants on farms and in workshops. Many Vikings were slave-traders. Prisoners who had been captured on raids all over Europe were sold as thralls. Viking society allowed thralls few rights. Their children were slaves as well.

The most powerful and wealthy Vikings were chieftains or *jarls* (earls). They controlled large areas of countryside. Some jarls even became local kings. Viking kings became more and more powerful as they built up new, united countries. By 900, Harald Finehair, King of Vestfold, had managed to bring all of Norway under his control. Denmark, however, had always been ruled by a single person. In the reign of Harald Bluetooth, the country became more centralized than ever.

Yet the early Vikings had been independent, quarrelsome and proud people, and this remained true in colonies such as Iceland. Many people, including Eirik the Red, had fled there to escape the law back home. They did not like the idea of being ruled by kings from far away. Iceland remained an independent republic throughout the whole of the Viking Age. After 1100, however, it was forced to recognize a Norwegian king.

STRONG RULERS
This king is a piece in a chess set from the Isle of Lewis, Scotland. Viking kings were often violent men who were hungry for power. They led their men into battle and fought with them to the bitter end.

THE FIGHTING KARLS
Karls, or freemen, formed the backbone of a Scandinavian invasion force when the Normans attacked England in 1066. This scene is part of the Bayeux tapestry and shows Norman karls preparing for conquest.

FARMERS
Viking karls, or freemen, built farmhouses on the Shetland islands to the north of Scotland. The search for new land to farm led many karls to travel overseas. The buildings on Shetland were made of timber, stone and turf. Confusingly, this Viking site is known as Jarlshof today.

LOYAL TO YOUR LORD

This reconstruction of a Viking raid is taking place on the island of Lindisfarne in northern England. Viking raiders first attacked Lindisfarne in the year 793. A typical war band would have been made up of free men, or karls. In battle, the karls followed their jarl, or earl, into the thick of the fighting without hesitation. They formed a tight guard around him when the fighting got tough. In the early Viking days, it was more important to show loyalty to one's family or lord than to a kingdom.

DEFENSIVE FORT

King Harald Bluetooth had a series of forts built to defend the Danish kingdom in the 980s. This one is at Fyrkat, in Jutland. By the end of the Viking period, the days of independent Viking chieftains leading a small band of karls on a raid had all but disappeared.

quadrant

rampart

entrance

communal hall

A RESTLESS PEOPLE

Poor farmhands prepare wool in this reconstruction showing Vikings at work. Families of all social classes left Scandinavia to settle new lands during the Viking age. They were driven by the need for land and wealth. They faced long sea voyages and years of hard work building new farms or towns.

Laws and Assemblies

LAWS AND JUDGEMENTS WERE passed at a public assembly called the *Thing*. This met region by region, and also in the lands where the Vikings settled. The assembly met at regular intervals and was made up only of free men. Women and slaves had no right to speak there.

The Thing had great powers, and could even decide who should be king. If someone was murdered or robbed, the victim's relatives could go to the Thing and demand justice. Everybody in the assembly considered the case. If they all agreed that a person was guilty, then judgement was passed. The person sentenced might have to pay a fine of money or other valuable goods. Sometimes the only way the dispute could be settled was by mortal combat – a fight to the death. However, mortal combat was itself made illegal in Iceland and Norway around AD1000. The assembly also dealt with arguments over property, marriage and divorce.

In Iceland there was no king at all in the Viking period. Instead, an *Althing* or national assembly was held each midsummer. The Althing was a cross between a court, a parliament and a festival. It was a chance for families to come in from their isolated farmhouses and meet up with each other. The assembly approved laws that had been drafted by the jarls and elected a Law Speaker.

PAY UP
The Thing could order a criminal to pay the victim, in the form of money or goods. If the criminal failed to do so, he was made an outlaw. This entitled anyone to kill him.

THE PLACE OF LAWS
The Icelandic Althing met on the Thingvellir, a rocky plain to the east of Reykjavik. A Law Speaker read out the laws, which had been passed by a group of 39 chieftains, from the Law Rock. The Althing is the world's oldest surviving law-making assembly on record. It met from 930 until 1800 and again from 1843. Today it is Iceland's parliament.

A DIFFICULT DECISION

This carving shows an important gathering of the Althing in 1000. The assembly was split over a difficult decision – should Iceland become Christian? It was left to the Law Speaker to decide. After a lot of thought, he ruled that the country should be officially Christian, but that people who wished to worship the old gods could do so in private.

MANX LAW

This earth mound marks the site of the old Viking assembly on the Isle of Man. The Vikings who settled on this island, off the west coast of Great Britain, called this assembly field the Tynwald. This is also the name of the island's parliament today. The Tynwald still has the power to make the island's laws.

MORTAL COMBAT

A Viking duel is re-enacted today. Life was cheap in Viking times and violent death was common. A fight to the death was an official way of settling a serious dispute, such as an accusation of murder. This system of justice was taken to England by the Normans in 1066.

LAW MAKERS

Viking chieftains would ride to Iceland's Thingvellir (Assembly Plain) from all over the island. This 19th-century painting by W G Collingwood shows chieftains assembling for the Althing. This assembly was held only once a year.

The Gods of Valholl

THE EARLY VIKINGS believed that the universe was held up by a great ash tree called Yggdrasil. The universe was made up of several separate worlds. Niflheim was the underworld, a misty realm of snow and ice. The upper world was Asgard, home of the gods. Its great hall was called Valholl (Valhalla), and it was here that warriors who died bravely in battle came to feast. The world of humans was called Midgard. It was surrounded by a sea of monsters and linked to Asgard by a rainbow bridge. Beyond the sea lay Utgard, the forest home of the Giants, deadly enemies of the gods.

The Vikings believed in many gods. They thought that Odin, father of the gods, rode through the night sky. Odin's wife was Frigg (a day of the week – Friday – is named after her) and his son was Baldr, god of the summer Sun. Powerful, red-bearded Thor was the god of thunder. Like many of the Vikings themselves, he enjoyed laughing, but was quick to anger. The twins Frey and Freya were god and goddess of fertility and love. Trouble was stirred up by Loki, a mischief-making god.

THOR'S HAMMER
This lucky charm from Iceland shows Thor. He used his magic hammer to fight the giants. Thor was strong and brave.

WORSHIPPING FREYA
This silver charm shows Freya. She was the goddess of love and marriage and was particularly popular in Sweden. Freya was the sister of Frey, the god of farming. It was also believed that when women died, Freya would welcome them into the next world. In *Egil's Saga*, a dying woman says 'I have not eaten and shall not till I am with Freya'.

BALDR IS SLAIN
Stories tell how the wicked Loki told the blind god Hod to aim a mistletoe spear at Baldr, god of the Sun and light.

MAKE A LUCKY CHARM

You will need: thick paper or card, pencil, scissors, self-hardening clay, board, felt-tipped pen, modelling tool, rolling pin, fine sandpaper, silver acrylic paint, brush, water pot, a length of cord.

1 Draw the outline of Thor's hammer onto thick paper or card and cut it out. Use this as the pattern for making your lucky charm, or amulet.

2 Place a lump of the clay on the board and roll it flat. Press your card pattern into the clay so that it leaves an outline of the hammer.

3 Remove the card. Use a modelling tool to cut into the clay. Follow around the edge of the imprint as shown, and peel away the hammer shape.

SLEIPNIR

Odin rode across the sky on Sleipnir, a grey, eight-legged horse. A pair of wolves travelled with Odin. In this carved stone from Sweden, Odin and Sleipnir are arriving at Valholl. They would have been welcomed by a *valkyrie*, or servant of the gods, bearing wine for Odin to drink.

Vikings wore lucky charms or amulets to protect themselves from evil. Many of the charms, such as this hammer, honoured the god Thor.

ODIN

One-eyed Odin was the wisest of all gods. He had two ravens called Hugin, meaning 'thought', and Mugin, meaning 'memory'. Each day the ravens flew across the world. Every evening they flew back to Odin to perch on his shoulders and report to him the deeds that they had seen.

4 Model a flattened end to the hammer, as shown. Use a modelling tool to make a hole at the end, to thread the cord through when it is dry.

5 Use the end of a felt-tipped pen, a pencil or modelling tool to press a series of patterns into the clay, as shown. Leave to dry and harden.

6 When the amulet is dry, smooth any rough edges with sandpaper. Paint one side silver. Leave it to dry before painting the other side.

7 When the paint has dried, take enough cord to fit your neck and thread it through the hole in the hammer. Cut it with the scissors and tie a knot.

The Coming of Christianity

BY THE BEGINNING of the Viking Age, most of western Europe had become Christian. The early Vikings despised the Christian monks for being meek and mild. The warriors looted church treasures on their raids and murdered many priests or sold them into slavery. However, over the years, some Vikings found it convenient to become Christian. This made it easier for them to trade with merchants in western Europe and to hire themselves out as soldiers with Christian armies.

Christian missionaries went to Scandinavia from Germany and the British Isles. Monks from Constantinople preached to the Vikings living in the Ukraine and Russia. They soon gained followers. In about 960, King Harald Bluetooth of Denmark became a Christian. In 995, Olaf Tryggvason, a Christian king, came to the throne of Norway. He pulled down many of the shrines to the old gods. In 1000 the Viking colonists on Iceland also voted to become Christian. The new faith spread from there to Greenland. Sweden was the last Viking country to become Christian. People gave up worshipping pagan gods in the old temples of the settlement at Uppsala.

NEW FAITH
This silver crucifix was found in the Gotland region of Sweden. It is nearly 1,000 years old. It shows Christ wearing breeches, like those worn by Viking men.

STAVE CHURCH
This Christian church is made of staves, or split tree trunks. It was built in Gol, in Norway, in about 1200. The very first Christian churches in Scandinavia were built in this way. When the wooden foundations rotted away, the churches were rebuilt.

SIGN OF THE CROSS
This stone was raised at Jelling in Denmark by King Harald Bluetooth, in honour of his parents. It dates from about 985. The stone marks a turning-point in Viking history – the conversion of the Danes to Christianity. One side of the stone shows a dragon-like beast fighting with a snake. The other side is a Christian scene (*above*), showing Jesus on the cross.

crucifix

CHOICE OF GODS

The mould below was made from a soft mineral called soapstone. It was used to shape metal pendants 1,000 years ago. The mould could produce both hammer-of-Thor designs and crosses (*above*). The two religions – the old and the new – existed side-by-side for many years in the Viking world. It was a long time before Christianity really took hold. Many of the early converts to Christianity still turned to Thor for help in the heat of battle.

Thor's hammer charms

mould

BAPTISM IN A BARREL

The Danish king, Harald Bluetooth, was converted to Christianity in about 960. This gold altar piece shows Harald being baptized in a barrel of holy water by Bishop Poppo. Harald went on to build a Christian church on the ancient site of the royal burial mound at Jelling.

AGAINST EVIL

Is this a silver cross, or a hammer-of-Thor charm with a dragon's head? Perhaps it was both. It was certainly intended to protect the wearer from evil and bad luck. Even after they became Christians, the Vikings remained very superstitious people. Helgi the Lean is described in a Viking saga as believing in Christ 'yet he still asked Thor for help on sea voyages and when facing danger'.

STONE CROSS

This cross is from Kirkinner Church, in Scotland. It is about 1,000 years old. Its carving shows a mixture of Anglian and Norwegian Viking styles. The Christians in Britain, France and Germany were horrified by the Vikings' pagan religion, and they tried to persuade them to give it up. Eventually, Viking kings saw that becoming Christian could make them more powerful.

Settlements and Towns

HEDEBY
This is a model of Hedeby, an important market town, now in modern Germany. This area used to be part of Denmark. At its peak in 950, Hedeby was home to over 1,000 people.

THE WORLD in which the Vikings lived was not as crowded as ours. Many families lived in farmhouses far from anyone else. Some lived in small settlements on the shores of remote deep sea inlets called *fjords*. The Vikings built small towns when they settled new lands or set up trading posts. These towns were usually ranged around a waterfront by the sea or a river, where ships could moor for loading. The smell of fish would hang in the air, accompanied by the sound of squabbling gulls. Away from the waterfront, the town would usually be defended by a ring of earthworks and wooden stockades. It might be attacked at any time.

Viking merchants' town houses were often built of timber planks or of wattle and daub (a criss-cross design of sticks covered with clay or dung). Houses had fenced yards or gardens, where chickens, geese and pigs were kept. Fresh water came from wells and springs. The streets were lined with market stalls selling goods. They were unpaved, but lengths of timber were laid down to stop them getting too muddy. Rubbish was thrown onto a midden or tip. There was no proper drainage. Towns must have been unhealthy and smelly places. Sewage went straight into holes dug in the ground or it was dumped in a large pit called a cesspit.

WALLS OF STONE
Building materials depended on local supply. These stone ruins mark the outlines of an ancient Viking settlement on the Brough of Birsay. This tiny island lies on the shores of mainland Orkney, whose Viking name means 'island of seals'. The Orkney islands, off the north coast of Scotland, were settled by the Vikings from the year 800.

houses built back from the street but facing towards it

store house

settlement built around a stream

timber-framed houses with panels of wattle, daubed with dung or clay to make them waterproof

most houses in the settlement would be thatched with reed

settlement situated in a natural harbour, providing sheltered accommodation

jetty for loading and unloading cargo

merchants' and craftsmen's plots fenced

LIVING IN TOWNS

This is how a Viking settlement might have looked 1,100 years ago. There are houses of various sizes. A merchant's house, for example, could cover an area of about 90 square metres/270 square feet. Sometimes there were also workshops or warehouses. Servants and slaves lived in small huts, which were often damp or draughty.

TURF CONSTRUCTION

In countryside settlements, timbers or stones were often covered with a thick layer of turf. This acted as the roof and walls. These Viking farmhouses have been rebuilt at Glaumber, in Iceland.

UNCOVERING A TOWN

Archaeologists excavate a Viking town house at the settlement of Jorvik (York), in England. The oldest houses in Jorvik were made of wattle, twigs tightly woven around upright posts. Oak planks were used in later Viking buildings. The stones in the foreground are part of an old hearth.

The Longhouse

THE MOST TYPICAL Viking houses were farmsteads, built in the countryside. At the centre of the farming settlement was a large building called the longhouse. This was a low building up to 30m/90ft in length, which was usually built of timber. Stone boulders were used on islands, such as Iceland, where there was a shortage of trees. Roofs were thatched or covered with a layer of turf.

Early in the Viking Age, longhouses were basic. Family and farmworkers lived together in a single great hall. There was even a section for the animals under the same roof. People huddled around the central fire to keep warm. Later, longhouses often had extra rooms, such as a bedroom for the farmer and his wife, a room for spinning and weaving wool, and a dairy where the women made butter and cheese. There was sometimes a separate kitchen, a food store and a bath house. Toilets were simple earth pits dug off the main hall. Outbuildings included byres and barns where the animals were kept in winter. Farm tools and weapons were repaired in a workshop.

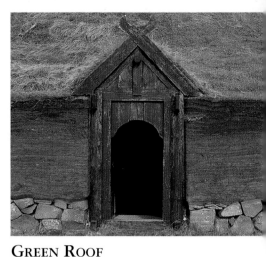

GREEN ROOF
This reconstructed Icelandic home has wattle-and-daub walls. The roof is covered with thick strips of turf, to keep out the cold. The grass on the roof turf keeps growing.

DANISH DWELLING
This longhouse was reconstructed at Trelleborg in Denmark. It is similar to the style of the fortress longhouses that stood here in 900. These buildings had long, curved roofs covered in wooden tiles. Historians now believe that the pillars on this reconstruction are not accurate.

MAKE A HOUSE

You will need: thick card, ruler, pencil, scissors, balsa wood, craft (utility) knife, paintbrushes, brown, white and black acrylic paints, masking tape, PVA (white) glue, brush, straw, sandpaper.

10cm/4in
7cm/2¾in
front door

To decorate: 12 x strips of balsa wood 6–7cm/2½–2¾in long.

walls x 2
6cm/2½in
14cm/5½in

15cm/6in
roof
5.5cm/2⅛in

back
7cm/2¾in
10cm/4in
10cm/4in
base
20cm/8in
10cm/4in

Ask an adult to cut out thick card pieces house using the measurements above (templates not shown to scale).

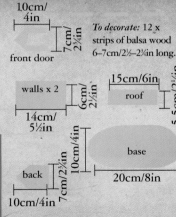

1 Paint all the walls of the house brown and leave them to dry. Using a piece of card as a guide, pick out the wattle-and-daub pattern with white paint.

2 Paint in wooden planking above the door and leave to dry. Stick balsa wood strips around the door and gables and on the side walls, as shown.

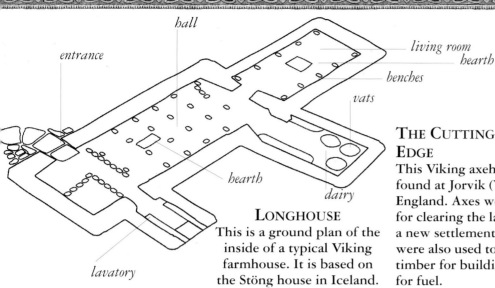

entrance

hall

living room
hearth

benches

vats

hearth

dairy

lavatory

LONGHOUSE

This is a ground plan of the inside of a typical Viking farmhouse. It is based on the Stöng house in Iceland.

THE CUTTING EDGE

This Viking axehead was found at Jorvik (York) in England. Axes were used for clearing the land for a new settlement. They were also used to fell timber for building and for fuel.

HARD WORK

In the Viking Age there was no machinery to help people build houses and barns. Everything depended on muscle power. Timber had to be chopped down and shaped with an axe. Stones had to be quarried and hauled to the site. Reeds for the thatch were cut and gathered. Turf for roofs was dug from moorlands and bogs.

turf

timber

stone

straw

HOME FROM HOME

This is where Eirik the Red and his wife Thjodhild built their Greenland longhouse from stone over 1,000 years ago. Life in the Greenland settlements was very harsh.

The Vikings adapted to their surroundings by using whatever materials were available locally for their houses. In Denmark, wood was used. However, in Greenland stone was more plentiful.

3 Paint the base brown and allow to dry thoroughly. Glue the walls in position on the base. Use masking tape to secure them while the glue dries.

4 Tape layers of straw thatch onto the roof section. (Instead of using real straw you could chop off the bristles from a decorating brush.)

5 Finish off the roof. Continue building up layers of thatch with straw. Make sure that the layers are even to give the roof a good finish.

6 Stick on the thatch roof. Tear sandpaper into pieces and glue onto the base to look like rough turf. Glue balsa strips on to the base as a pathway.

Inside a Viking Home

THE LIGHT WAS DIM inside a Viking house. There might be just one small window with wooden shutters and no glass. The air indoors would have been sharp with smoke from burning logs or a peat fire. The fire burned in a central hearth made from stone. There were no chimneys, so the smoke from the fire drifted out through a hole in the roof.

In the houses of wealthy families, the wooden walls and beams were sometimes beautifully carved. Tapestries might hang on the walls, but there were no carpets. Instead, sweet-smelling rushes were scattered on the earth floor. They were swept away when they became soiled. Built-in ledges around the walls were used for sitting on by day and sleeping on by night. In later times, rich people might have owned a special bed, which would have been finely carved. Mattresses were filled with down or with straw. The bed covers were woollen blankets or warm furs.

There was much less furniture than in a typical modern home. Weapons, tools and clothes were hung from the wall or stored in large chests. Jewellery or money could be hidden away in strongboxes or caskets. Foodstuffs, such as butter, salted fish or flour and drinks, such as ale, were stored in buckets, barrels and tubs.

FLICKERING LIGHT
Small lamps were placed on tables or hung from the ceiling. They were carved from soapstone and filled with oil and a wick. Working indoors was hard. A lamp like this would have given out poor light that flickered in the breeze.

CENTRAL HEARTH
This picture of a 100-year-old hearth shows how cauldrons of hot food would have simmered over the fire in an Icelandic farmhouse. The hearth was at the centre of every Viking home, providing light and warmth.

MAKE A DRINKING HORN

You will need: thick paper, pencil, ruler, scissors, mug, masking tape, brown paper, self-hardening clay, newspaper, water, PVA (white) glue and brush, paints, brush, silver foil.

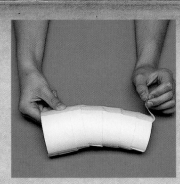

1 Cut the paper into strips 28cm/11in in length, but different widths. Roll the widest into a ring using the rim of a mug as a guide. Bind the edges with tape.

2 Next roll up the next widest strip, and bind it with tape. Place it inside the first. Make more rings, each one slightly smaller than the previous one.

3 Place each of the smaller rings into the slightly larger one before it, binding with tape. You are making the tapered shape of a curved horn.

ROYAL BED

A princess or queen slept in this fine bed. It was found in a ship buried in Norway. Only the rich would have had beds and separate bedrooms. Ordinary people slept on benches spread with rugs.

LOCK UP YOUR LOOT!

Keys, such as these, were used to lock a chest. This is where a Viking would have kept precious things, such as daggers or silver.

AT HOME IN YORK

This is a reconstruction of a Viking home in Jorvik. Baskets and bags hang from the ceiling and a large barrel sits in the corner. An old man warms himself by the hearth. No doubt he is telling tales of exciting sea voyages in his youth, or complaining about his aches and pains!

Viking drinking horns were filled for a toast with mead, a drink made from honey, water and yeast.

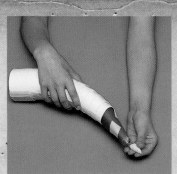

4 Roll the brown paper into a cone to make the horn's pointed end, and bind it in position. Round off the sharp end with clay. Leave it to dry and harden.

5 Cover the horn in papier mâché. Cut strips of newspaper, soak them in water and glue them to the horn. Leave to dry and then add more layers.

6 When the papier mâché is dry, paint the horn. To look real, the main part of the horn should be white, with the tip painted brown and black.

7 Cut the silver foil into a pattern and glue it to the rim of the horn. Real Viking drinking horns were often beautifully decorated with silver.

Family Life

E VEN IN MODERN ICELAND, everybody seems to
know who is related to whom and where they
live. In Viking times too, a large number of
relatives played their part in the family, including
grandparents, aunts and uncles. They were all very
aware of family links, and loyalty was fierce. If one
member of a family was harmed, then the other
members of the family would seek revenge. This
led to feuds – quarrels between one family and
another that simmered on from one generation to
the next. Feuds led to fights, theft and sometimes
even murder.

The father of the household had great power over
other members of the family. If he thought a
newborn baby was a weakling, he could leave it
to die. When a Viking
farmer died, his eldest
son inherited the farm.
The rest of the family
would have to move
away, and the
younger sons

HELPING OUT
This reconstruction of a market stall in Jorvik shows a
young lad helping his parents during a day's trading.
Children often followed in the same trade as their
parents. This boy would have learned how to haggle
over prices. He would also know how to weigh silver.

would have to find new land of their own to farm. Mothers were
often strong, determined women who had great influence in the
family. There was little schooling. Learning how to fight with a
sword or use an axe was more important than reading and writing.
As children grew up, they were expected to work hard and to help
around the house. They were sometimes fostered out to families
on other farms and had to work in return for their keep.

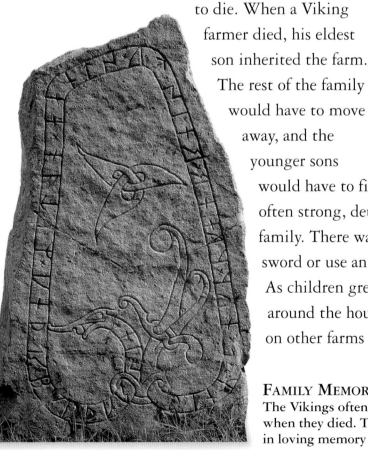

FAMILY MEMORIALS
The Vikings often put up memorial stones to honour relatives and friends
when they died. This stone from Sweden was put up by Tjagan and Gunnar
in loving memory of their brother Vader.

LIVING IN FEAR

Old tales tell how Vikings fought each other mercilessly during long, bitter feuds between families. Murderous bands might turn up at a longhouse by night, threatening to burn down the roof and kill everybody inside. Viking households also risked attack from local peoples or other raiders wherever they settled.

WANTING CHILDREN

A woman who wanted to make a good marriage and have children would pray to Frey, the god of love and fertility. On these gold foil charms from Sweden, Frey is shown with his beautiful wife Gerda. She was the daughter of a giant called Gymir.

BURIAL GRAVE

This skeleton belongs to a Viking woman from Iceland. Archaeologists have been able to tell how women lived in the Viking age by examining the goods placed in their graves. These were possessions for them to use in the next world.

GROWING UP

Children were expected to work hard in Viking times. Boys were taught farming, rowing and sailing. Girls were taught how to spin and weave, milk cows and prepare food. When all the daily tasks had been done, boys probably played games or went fishing. Viking girls may have spent some of their free time gathering berries and mushrooms.

Viking Women

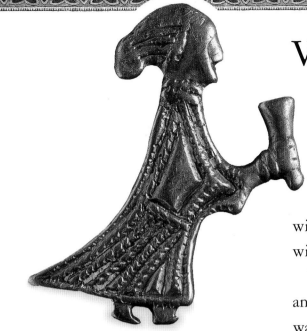

WELCOME HOME
A woman in typical Viking dress welcomes a warrior returning from the wars. She has long hair tied back by a scarf and is wearing a pleated dress. The woman is a valkyrie, one of Odin's maidens in Valholl. This charm comes from Öland in Sweden.

VIKING WOMEN could not speak at the assembly, yet they had more independence than many European women of their day. They could choose their own husband, own property and be granted a divorce. At a wedding, both the bride and groom had to make their marriage vows before witnesses. Memorial stones show that many husbands loved their wives and treated them with respect.

Women certainly needed to be tough in the harsh landscapes and cold climates of countries such as Iceland or Greenland. It was their job to make woollen or linen clothes for the family, to prepare and cook food and to clean the home.

It was the women who usually had to manage the farm and its workers while their men were off raiding or trading. They never knew if their husbands, brothers and sons would return from the wars in the British Isles or be lost in a storm at sea.

A DAY'S WORK
In this reconstruction from Jorvik (York), a Viking woman goes out to fetch water from the well. Hissing geese beat their wings and scatter in her path. Women's work lasted from dawn till nightfall, with clothes to darn, poultry to look after, meals to cook and children to scold! Most women also spent several hours a day spinning and weaving wool into cloth to make clothes.

PRACTICAL BUT PRETTY

Viking women wore long tunics fastened by a pair of brooches. This Viking brooch was found in Denmark. It is over 1,000 years old and is made of gold. Women wore clothing that was both practical and comfortable.

GETTING READY

Before a wedding or a visit to the fair, a Viking woman may have smoothed or pleated her dress on a board like this one. A glass ball would have been used instead of an iron. This whalebone board comes from Norway.

WEAVING AT HOME

Viking looms were like this one. The warps, or upright threads, hang from a crossbar. The weft, or cross threads, pass between them to make cloth. Weaving was done by women in every Viking home.

THE NEW QUEEN

This picture shows Queen Aelfgyfu alongside her husband King Cnut, in England. Aelfgyfu was Cnut's second wife. They are placing a cross on an altar. Queens were the most powerful women in Scandinavian society.

BELOVED WIFE

This stone was put up by King Gorm as a monument to his wife. The inscription reads 'King Gorm made this memorial to his wife Thyri, adornment of Denmark'. The messages written on such stones show the qualities that Vikings admired most in women.

Dress and Decoration

TYPICAL DRESS FOR Viking women and girls was a long shift. It was made of wool or linen. Over this they wore a woollen tunic, with shoulder straps secured by ornate brooches. Between the brooches there was often a chain or a string of beads. Sometimes a chain dangled by their side, holding keys. Men and boys wore long breeches and knee-length woollen tunics with sleeves. Brightly coloured clothes were popular with both sexes.

Trade with Asia brought richer cloths, such as fine silk, to the Viking homelands. Woollen cloaks and caps were worn to keep out the winter cold. Shoes and boots were flat and made of leather. Viking men often wore beards. Both men and women had their hair long. Hair could be tied back with a band. Women often plaited (braided) or knotted their hair, or tucked it under a headscarf.

HAIR CARE
Both Viking men and women took great care of their long, flowing hair. The combs they used were often made of horn from the antlers of red deer. Many combs were beautifully carved.

BOOTS AND SHOES
Viking cobblers made slippers, shoes and boots of calfskin or goatskin. Footwear was often laced with a leather thong. New soles were sewn on when the old ones were completely worn through. These shoes were discovered in the city of Jorvik (York).

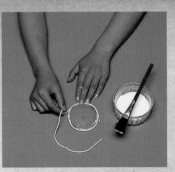

The Vikings loved showy jewellery, especially rings, armbands and gold and silver necklaces. These were often decorated with ornate designs. Jewellery was a sign of wealth and could be used instead of money to buy things.

MAKE A BROOCH
You will need: self-hardening clay, rolling board, string, PVA (white) glue and brush, bronze paint, water, brush, compasses, tracing paper, pencil, ruler, gold foil, scissors, card, safety pin.

1 Take a ball of clay and mould it into a brooch shape, as shown. The brooch should be 2–3cm/ ¾–1¼in in diameter. Leave it in a warm place to dry.

2 Place glue round the edge of the brooch and carefully stick string around outside as shown. This will make a border for the Viking brooch.

3 When the brooch is dry, paint it carefully with bronze acrylic paint. Paint the string border, too. Leave the brooch in a warm place to dry.

PRECIOUS AMBER

Amber is a transparent pine resin. The resin hardened into a fossil in prehistoric times. Its beautiful shades of gold, yellow and brown made it popular with Viking jewellers. They also used tinted glass for making fine bead necklaces.

amber

glass

GOLD AND JEWELS

This hoard of gold and jewels was hidden away in Norway in the 800s. It includes fine rings and necklaces and other precious items from France, England and Arab countries. Most of it would have been looted or raided. Such items were sometimes worn, or melted down for sale.

BURIED SILVER

This beautiful Viking brooch was found in a hoard buried in northern England. It is over 1,000 years old and is made of silver. Brooches were used to fasten cloaks and dresses.

SOCKS

This Viking sock was found at Jorvik (York). Cloth and fabric is not found very often because these materials usually rot more quickly than metal or stone. The few items that have been found were preserved in waterlogged soil.

Brooches were important pieces of jewellery – and not only for decoration! They were used as fasteners for cloaks and tunics.

4 Use a pair of compasses to draw two brooch-sized circles on paper. Draw a common Viking pattern in your circles or trace one from a book.

5 Trace the patterns on to a piece of gold foil. Take care not to tear the foil. Cut the patterns out in small pieces that will interlink.

6 Glue the interlinking pieces of foil on to the outside of one of the brooches and leave to dry. Repeat in the same way with the other brooch.

7 Cut and stick a circle of card on to the back of each brooch. Fix a safety pin to the back of each brooch with masking tape. Your brooch is now ready!

Farming and Fishing

THE VIKINGS ARE so famous as warriors and pirates that we sometimes forget that they mostly lived by farming and fishing. Their best farmland lay in Denmark and southern Sweden. Viking settlers overseas had to make do with some very poor soils and harsh climates. Pigs and poultry were kept in most farmyards. Viking farmers also raised sheep, goats and cattle. In Norway, herds of cows were led to mountain pastures during the summer and brought down to the farmstead for the winter. Many cattle were slaughtered as winter set in and their meat was preserved by salting, drying or smoking. Crops grown by Viking farmers included grains such as wheat, barley and oats. Flax was grown in warmer regions, such as Denmark, and was made into linen. Farm tools were home-made from wood and iron, and included hoes, picks, shovels, scythes, sickles and shears. Thralls, or slaves, toiled away clearing forests, digging, threshing and harvesting.

VIKING PONIES

These tough little ponies are from Iceland. The ponies that were bred by the Vikings in Iceland, the Shetland Isles and northern Scandinavia grew a warm winter coat. They grazed on turf and were fed hay in the winter. They were used for carrying peat and other heavy loads, and for riding.

HARVEST OF THE SEA

Fishermen used both nets and barbed metal fish hooks, such as these, to snare their catch. All kinds of freshwater fish could be had from lakes and rivers. The Baltic Sea, North Sea and North Atlantic Ocean provided them with fish such as herring and cod. Fishbones found in Viking middens, or rubbish tips, show that fish formed a major part of the diet.

FISHING BOAT

Fishing scenes such as this would have been common in the fjords of Norway and along the coast of Iceland. This carving is from Cumbria in northern England. It shows the god Thor and the giant Hymir fishing for the serpent of Midgard.

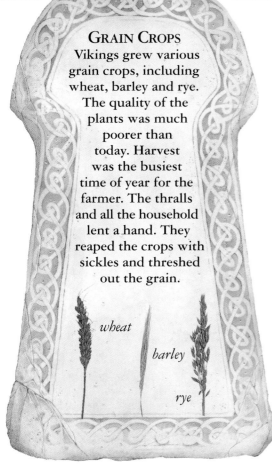

GRAIN CROPS

Vikings grew various grain crops, including wheat, barley and rye. The quality of the plants was much poorer than today. Harvest was the busiest time of year for the farmer. The thralls and all the household lent a hand. They reaped the crops with sickles and threshed out the grain.

wheat

barley

rye

HAVE YOU ANY WOOL?

This modern reconstruction from Jorvik (York) shows a Viking shepherd boy and his sheepdog, with a newly shorn fleece. Wool was the main fabric for cloth-making.

WORKING THE LAND

This springtime scene, embroidered on a wall hanging from Bayeux, Normandy, shows a man ploughing with horses and another sowing. Spring was the busiest time of year for the Viking farmer.

Food and Feasts

A VIKING FAMILY ate twice a day. The food was usually prepared at the central hearth, although some large farmhouses had separate kitchens. Chiefs held long, drunken feasts in their great halls, and wedding celebrations could go on for weeks.

Oats, barley and rye were made into bread and porridge. The hand-ground flour was often coarse and gritty and poor people added peas and bark to make it go further. The dough was mixed in large wooden troughs and then baked in ovens or on stone griddles. Goat, beef and horse meat were all popular and would be roasted over the fire or stewed in cauldrons. Hunting provided venison, reindeer, wild boar, wildfowl and hare. Honey was used to sweeten dishes, as sugar was still unknown in Europe. It was also used to make a strong alcoholic drink called mead. Wines were made from fruits and berries. Beer made from barley was gulped down from the hollowed-out horns of cattle.

VES HEILL!
'Be healthy!' was the toast in old Iceland. Vikings swigged their ale from drinking horns. These were often beautifully decorated with ornate metal bands.

BRING ME WINE!
A group of Norman lords drink wine from horns, in England in 1086. The Normans had invaded England 20 years before. They were descendants of Hrolf and the Vikings who had been given lands in France in 911. Norman life was still centred around the great hall in which banquets were held.

ON THE TABLE
Bowls and platters were made of wood. Spoons were made of horn or metal. People picked up meat in their fingers and cut it with a sharp knife or dagger – there were no forks.

MAKE A VIKING LOAF
You will need: sieve (strainer), bowl, 225g/8oz/2 cups white flour, 115g/4oz/1 cup wholemeal (whole-wheat) flour, 5ml/1 tsp baking powder, 5ml/1 tsp salt, 150g/5oz/1 cup seeds, wooden spoon, baking tray.

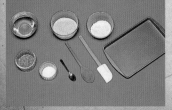

1 First wash your hands. Then begin by sifting together the white flour and the wholemeal flour through a sieve into a mixing bowl.

2 Sprinkle the baking powder and salt into the sifted flour. Adding a little bit of salt will help to give flavour to your Viking loaf.

3 Stir half of the seeds into the bowl. Sunflower seeds give a crunchy texture to the loaf, but you could use any other edible seeds.

VIKING TASTES

The quality of Viking vegetables was probably not as good as that of those available today. Cabbages and peas used by cooks were tough and stringy. Seeds, garlic and herbs, such as dill and coriander (cilantro), were used to add flavour to many dishes. Many of these herbs grew wild.

dill

coriander (cilantro)

DRINK IT UP!

These cups and jug (pitcher) would have been on the table of a merchant in the Swedish town of Birka. They may have held water, wine or mead. A lot of pottery was imported into Scandinavia from Germany and the lands to the south.

The Vikings used seeds and split peas to add flavour and bulk to bread. Sunflower seeds make a tasty modern substitute.

4 Add 475ml/16fl oz/
2 cups warm water and stir well with a wooden spoon. At this stage the mixture should become quite stiff and hard to stir!

5 Use your hands to knead the mixture into a stiff dough. Sprinkle some flour on to your hands, to stop the mixture sticking to them.

6 When the dough is well kneaded and no longer sticky, place it on a greased baking tray. Sprinkle the rest of your seeds on top of the loaf.

7 Put the baking tray in a cold oven. Set the oven to 190°C/375°F/Gas 5 and cook the bread for 1 hour. Heating the dough from cold will help it to rise.

Land Transport

IN THE VIKING AGE, roads were mostly in poor repair, or were little more than muddy tracks. The Vikings made roadways by sinking timbers into the ground. They often built causeways across marshy ground. In many areas it was quicker to travel around the coast by boat than to cross mountains or moors in poor weather. In northern lands, snow and ice made winter travel difficult, although the Vikings were highly skilled at overcoming icy conditions.

The Vikings were good at riding. They used horses for travel and transport as well as in battle. Horses carried baggage and pulled wheeled carts and covered wagons. Sledges were also used to carry goods. They could be hauled over grass or soil as well as ice and snow. Carts and sledges found in the Oseberg ship burial were beautifully carved. The ones used every day were probably much plainer. The Vikings used skis, skates and snowshoes for travelling cross-country in winter.

CARVED SLEDGE
No less than four wooden sledges were found in the grave of the Viking queen buried at Oseberg in Norway. They were designed to be pulled by a horse. Three of the sledges were richly decorated.

RIDING OFF TO WAR
This silver figure shows a Viking warrior on horseback, carrying a sword. It was found at the market town of Birka in Sweden and is over 1,000 years old. The Vikings were skilled horsemen.

RIDING TACKLE
During the Viking Age, stirrups arrived in Europe from Asia. They began to be widely used by horse riders. Other remains of riding tackle discovered by archaeologists have included spurs (*above*), saddles, bridles and harnesses. They were often beautifully made.

MAKE A SLEDGE

You will need: thick cardboard, ruler, pencil, craft (utility) knife, PVA (white) glue, brush, red acrylic paint, brush, brown cartridge (construction) paper, scissors, paper fasteners, masking tape, red string, fur fabric.

sledge ends x 2

strips of brown cartridge paper

optional supports x 2

base for runners 26cm/10¼in

4.5cm/1¾in

4.5cm/1¾in

4.5cm/1¾in

base of sledge

17cm/6½in

20cm/8in

sledge sides x 2

5cm/2in

5.5cm/2¼in

17cm/6½in

runners x 2

30cm/12in

supports x 3

corner struts x 4

5cm/2in

4.5cm/1¾in

2 x 30cm/12in strips of balsa wood

Draw the pieces on to card using the measurements above (templates not shown to scale). Ask an adult to cut them out with a craft knife.

1 Glue the four corner struts to the sledge side pieces and leave to dry. Paint both sides of each of the five pieces that will form the top of the sledge.

HORSE POWER

Surviving bridles and harnesses show how horses became more and more important to the Vikings. The descendants of the Vikings in northern France – the Normans – were among the first warriors on horseback in Europe.

WOODEN WAGONS

This royal wagon was found in the Oseberg ship burial. It is covered in rich carvings. Similar ones can be seen on a tapestry found at Oseberg. The upper bodies of wagons like these could be taken off the carriage. They were sometimes used as coffins.

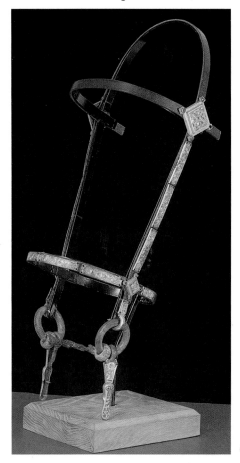

SITTING PRETTY

This is a saddle bow. It was found at Jorvik (York). It is decorated with silver and strips of horn. A bow is the raised ledge at the front and back of a saddle, which gives support to the rider.

Imagine a young Viking princess, wrapped in warm furs, riding over the snow and ice on a sledge like this.

2 Cut several strips of brown cartridge paper. Arrange the strips to form diamond patterns along the sides of the sledge. Trim them and glue in place.

3 Ask an adult to make holes with a pencil. Push paper fasteners through to form patterns. Glue the top of the sledge. Hold it together with masking tape.

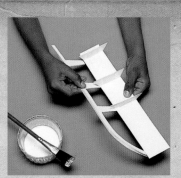

4 While you wait for the top to dry, glue the eight pieces that form the base of the sledge together. Glue the two supports on to strengthen the base.

5 Paint the base red and leave it to dry. When it is completely dry, brush plenty of glue down each side and carefully slide the top onto it. Leave it to dry.

All Kinds of Ship

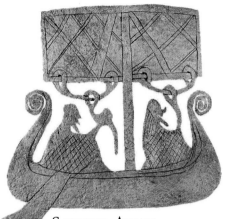

SAILING AWAY
This picture from a stone on Gotland, in Sweden, shows a small, two-man boat. Like larger Viking ships, it has a rectangular sail, a single mast and a broad steering oar towards the stern. The outlines of ropes and rigging can be made out, too.

CRESTING THE WAVES
The *knarr* was a trading vessel, designed for the open ocean. It had a covered deck at each end. The central hold could be filled to the brim with bales of wool. On board it might have had a small four-oared boat called a *færing*. This little boat could be used for a day's fishing in the fjord.

THE VIKINGS DEPENDED on the sea. It served as a highway for them. Ships were used for transport around the islands and fjords wherever they settled. Fish, seals and whales from the sea provided food, oil, skins and bone. The Vikings were masters at seafaring and were among the most skilful ship builders the world has ever seen.

The most famous Viking vessel was the longship. It could be up to 23m/70ft in length. This long, sleek sailing ship was used for ocean voyages and warfare. It was still shallow enough to row up a river. The longship had an open deck without cabins or benches. The rowers sat on hide-covered sea chests that contained their possessions, weapons and food rations. The Vikings built many other kinds of ship. They had broad-beamed ships for carrying cargoes up and down the coast, as well as small rowing and sailing boats for transport and fishing. The ships were all built to fine, curved designs, with high prows and sterns.

knarr

færing

MAKE A LONGSHIP
You will need: cardboard, pencil, ruler, scissors, paints, brush, water pot, balsa wood strips and pole, PVA (white) glue, brush, craft (utility) knife, masking tape, pale and dark brown paper, string.

14cm/5½in
supports x 3

Ask an adult to cut out the pieces of thick cardboard following the measurements shown below (templates not shown to scale).

35cm/14in balsa wood stick

30cm/12in balsa wood stick

balsa wood supports

6 x 14cm/5½in balsa wood strips

50cm/20in

28cm/11in

sail

19cm/7½in

2.5cm/1in

brown paper strips (lengths vary from 40–50cm/16–20in)

deck

14cm/5½in

48cm/19¼in

GOKSTAD SHIP
Royal ships have been excavated from Norwegian burial mounds at Gokstad and Oseberg. These funeral ships were beautifully made, but were not really designed for long ocean voyages.

BUILDING A FLEET
This is part of the Bayeux tapestry, from Normandy. It shows boats being built for the invasion of England in 1066. The Normans built ships the way their Viking ancestors would have done. Carpenters cut the oak planks with an axe and drilled them with a tool called an auger.

A ROYAL SHIP
This picture shows what the ship that was excavated from Gokstad would have looked like. Being a royal ship, it was built of the finest oak. It had a pine mast.

1 Paint the deck shape light brown on one side and black on the other. When it is dry, mark out the planks lengthwise 5mm/¼in apart.

2 Glue balsa wood cross support 'planks' onto the brown side of the deck as shown. Ask an adult to cut a hole in the deck with a craft knife, for the mast.

3 Turn the deck over. Measure and cut three more balsa wood planks. Glue them in position, matched with the planks on the other side.

4 Cut and glue three semicircular pieces of card for the crossbeams. *Instructions for making the ship continue on the next page...*

The Longship

VIKING LONGSHIPS WERE BUILT in the open air, on a beach or river shore. A single oak beam was used for the keel – the backbone of the ship. The keel was 18m/60ft or more in length. Iron nails and washers were used to fix the long, wedge-shaped planks to the frame. Longships were 'clinker-built', which means that each of the layers of planking, or strakes, overlapped the next. Another strong beam of wood supported the mast. This, together with the cross-beams, strengthened the frame of the boat. The planks were caulked (made watertight) with a stuffing of wool or animal hair. They were coated with a tar made of pine resin. Oar holes in the top strake ran the length of a longship. A broad steering oar was secured by thongs to the starboard (right-hand side) of the stern. The pine mast could be lowered. It supported a large square or rectangular sail made of heavy woollen or linen cloth. The sail was often patterned in stripes. The ship's simple rigging was made of hemp or sealskin ropes.

DRAGON SHIPS
The high prow of the Viking longship was often beautifully carved. This replica ship has a fierce dragon as its figurehead. Carvings like these were probably meant to scare off evil spirits. They certainly scared the enemy!

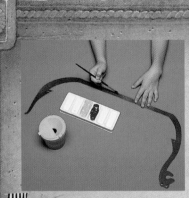

5 Carefully draw and cut out the pieces for the keel of the boat. Paint one side red and leave to dry. Then paint the other side of the keel.

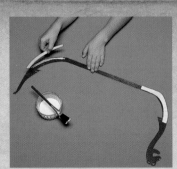

6 When the paint is completely dry, glue the pieces of balsa wood to the curved parts of the keel to strengthen them. Leave them to dry.

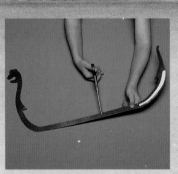

7 When the glue is dry, measure then make three slots along the length of the keel with a pair of scissors for the deck crossbeams to slot into.

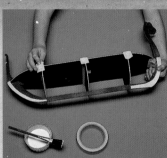

8 Slip the deck crossbeams into the slots on the keel pieces. Glue them in place. Bind them with masking tape to hold them while they dry.

MODERN VIKINGS

Modern ship builders have built replicas of longships, either for tourist voyages or to find out how well they sailed. These new longships have proved to be strong, fast and easy to sail. The planking bends well to the waves and is light enough for the ship to be hauled overland.

SHIPS' TIMBERS

In the Viking Age, much of northern Europe was still densely forested. In most places there was no shortage of timber for building or repairing longships. Oak was always the shipbuilders' first choice of wood, followed by pine, beech and ash.

beech

oak

PUTTING TO SEA

A longship put to sea with a crew of 30 or more fighting men. Each one would have to fight the enemy as well as man the oars. The warriors' round shields were sometimes slung or slotted along the side of the ship. An awning of sailcloth could be erected to keep off the sun or rain.

Journeys by longship could take their Viking crew far and wide.

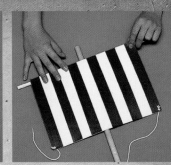

9 Cut strips of pale and dark brown paper for the planks, or 'strakes', along each side of the keel. Carefully glue a strip in position along each side.

10 Continue gluing strips in place. Alternate pale and dark brown strips. Trim the strips as they get lower so that they form a curve.

11 Ask an adult to help you to cut two pieces of balsa wood pole. Glue them together. When the glue is dry, bind them with string.

12 Cut out a square sail and paint it with red and white stripes. Glue it to the mast and attach some string rigging. Paint a dragon on the prow.

Seafaring and Navigation

ONGSHIPS WERE SPEEDY vessels. They were capable of sailing from Scandinavia to North America in under a month. Most voyages, however, were long and harsh and interrupted by storms and battles. There were supplies of fresh water on board. The food for the voyage included anything that could be easily stored, such as apples, cheese and dried meat. Fish could be caught along the way to provide fresh food for the sailors. Warriors usually slept on board the ship. Sometimes they ran the ship on to the beach and camped on shore. The Vikings understood winds, currents and tides better than any other seafarers in Europe at that time. When possible, they followed coastlines with known landmarks. When they crossed open ocean, they had to steer their ships by the Sun and stars. They often sketched out simple maps of coastlines and landmarks to use as charts for their long voyages.

Longships were often blown off course by storms. This was how the Vikings first discovered North America. A seafarer called Gunnbjorn was blown within sight of Greenland in about 920. This was 60 years before it was colonized by Eirik the Red. The Canadian coast was discovered by accident in about 985 by a lost seafarer called Bjarni Herjolfsson. This was 17 years before the expedition of Leif Eiriksson, known as Leif the Lucky.

A FAIR WIND
Gilded bronze weather vanes, like this one, topped the mast of many Viking ships. Sailors watched them for a change in the wind direction. This vane was later set up on the roof of a Swedish church.

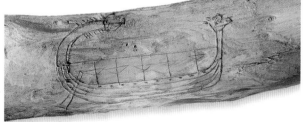

VIKING GRAFFITI
This sketch of a dragon-headed longship was scratched on to wood by an unknown Viking. Today it is in the National Maritime Museum at Bergen, in Norway.

MAKE A WIND VANE
You will need: stiff cardboard, pencil, pair of compasses, ruler, bradawl, gold acrylic paint, paintbrush, water pot, brass hinges, balsa wood, wood screws, screwdriver, gold card, PVA (white) glue, brush.

1 Draw a line across the cardboard. Draw a shorter vertical line at a right angle. Use a pair of compasses to draw the curved shape of the vane.

2 Cut out the wind vane, then use a bradawl to score lines in the card. Make up your own Viking pattern or copy the one shown here.

3 Cover the work surface to protect it. Paint the patterned card with a light, even layer of gold paint on one side. Leave it to dry. Paint the other side.

OUT OF THE STORM

This painting shows a Viking invasion fleet running before a strong wind across the North Sea. The awnings are raised against the driving rain and salt spray. Fleets of longships could be large. It was said that 300 of them could anchor in the harbour of the Jomsberg Viking fortress in Denmark.

A SAILOR'S PROVISIONS

Along with his best sword and a warm woollen cloak, a Viking warrior would have taken his own rations on board ship. He would have needed enough food to survive a storm or shipwreck – perhaps some smoked bacon, nuts, fish, a cask of ale and some hard cheese.

cheese

nuts

bacon

herrings

THE VINLAND MAP

This map includes Europe, North Africa, Greenland and Vinland, the area known now as Newfoundland. The Vinland map is said to have been copied in about 1440 from an original Viking map. However, most experts believe this map is a fake, produced in modern times.

A wind vane would have been fixed at the top of the longship's mast.

 **4** Place the hinges under the short border of the card. Push the point of the bradawl through the hinges, boring four holes through the card.

5 Cut a balsa wood mast. Ask an adult to help you to screw the wind vane to the mast using the brass hinges and some wood screws.

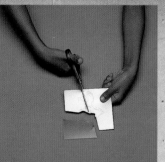 **6** Draw the shape of a real or imaginary bird or animal, such as a raven or dragon, on to the back of some gold card. Cut it out carefully.

7 Glue the gold bird or animal to the upper edge of the vane. Leave it to dry. Your Viking wind vane is ready and now all you need is a good breeze!

Traders and Merchants

COINS
These silver coins were found on the site of the market place in Birka. They were minted in Hedeby in around 800.

MAKING MONEY
This disc is a die – a metal stamp used to punch the design on to the face of a coin. The die is from York, in England. It has a sword design.

THE VIKINGS were second to none as successful merchants. Their home trade was based in towns such as Hedeby in Denmark, Birka in Sweden and Kaupang in Norway. As they settled new lands, their trading routes began to spread far and wide. They traded in countries as far apart as Britain, Iceland and Greenland.

In about 860 Swedish Vikings opened up new routes eastwards through the lands of the Slavs. They rowed and sailed down rivers such as the Volga, Volkhov and Dniepr. Viking sailors hauled their boats around rapids and fought off attacks from local peoples. Their trade turned the cities of Holmgard (Novgorod) and Könugard (Kiev) into powerful states. This marked the birth of Russia as a nation. Merchants crossed the Black Sea and the Caspian Sea. They travelled on to Constantinople (Istanbul), capital of the Byzantine empire, and to the great Arab city of Baghdad.

Viking warehouses were crammed with casks of wine from Germany and bales of woollen cloth from England. There were furs and walrus ivory from the Arctic and timber and iron from Scandinavia. Vikings also traded in wheat from the British Isles and rye from Russia.

AMBER KING
This carved amber king is a piece from a board game. Amber was exported from the lands around the Baltic Sea. It was much prized by traders and by craftworkers, who also made it into jewellery and lucky charms.

MAKE A COIN AND DIE

You will need: self-hardening clay and tool, board, rolling pin, scissors, pair of compasses, pencil, paper, PVA (white) glue, brush, paintbrush, bronze and silver paint.

1 Roll out a large cylinder of clay and model a short, thick handle at one end. This is the die. Leave it in a warm place to harden and dry.

2 Cut out a circle from paper. It should be about the same size as the end of the die. Draw a simple shape on the paper circle, with a pencil.

3 Cut the paper circle in half. Cut out the shape as shown. If you find it hard to cut the shape out, you could ask an adult to cut it out with a craft knife.

EASTERN CONNECTIONS

Trade networks in the East linked up with older routes, such as the 'silk road' to China. Silk, jewels and spices were brought by camel from the Far East. In Baghdad's markets, Vikings bought these things in return for furs, beeswax and slaves.

beeswax

silk

TRADE MAP

The routes taken by Viking traders fanned out south and east from their homelands. As well as exotic goods from the East, everyday items such as salt, pottery and wool were brought back from western Europe.

The first coins to show Viking kings were minted in England.

FAIR TRADING

Scales and weights were used by merchants wherever they traded. Some could be folded up inside a small case.

scales

scales

weights

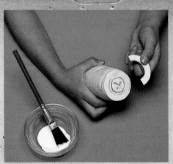

4 Glue the cut paper pieces onto the end of the die with PVA glue. You may need to trim the pieces if they are too big to fit on the end.

5 Viking dies would have been made of bronze, or some other metal. Paint your die a bronze colour. Make sure you paint an even coat.

6 Roll out some more clay. Use the die to stamp an impression into the clay. This is your first coin. You can make as many as you like.

7 Use a modelling tool to cut around the edge of the coin. Make more coins from the left-over clay. Let the coins harden and dry and then paint them silver.

Raids and Piracy

IN 793 A BAND of heavily armed Vikings ran their longships ashore on Lindisfarne (an island off the coast of Northumbria, in England). This was the site of a Christian monastery. The monks tried in vain to hide their precious crosses, their silver chalices and Bibles. The Vikings axed them down, set fire to the buildings and sailed away with their loot.

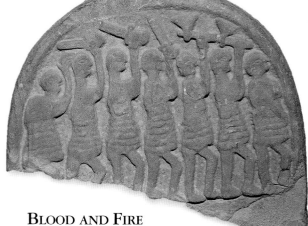

BLOOD AND FIRE
This gravestone is from Lindisfarne. It shows fierce Viking warriors armed with swords and battle axes.

This was the start of the period in which the Vikings spread terror around western Europe. They began by attacking easy targets, such as villages, monasteries, or other ships. They took away cattle or grain, chests of money and church bells that could be melted down. They also took women and slaves. The booty was shared out among members of the crew.

Soon the Vikings were attacking the largest and richest cities in Europe. In 846 they sacked, or raided, the cities of Hamburg, Germany and Paris, France. King Charles the Bald of France had to pay the Viking leader Ragnar Hairy-Breeks over three tonnes of silver to leave. From 865 onwards the English kings were also forced to pay huge sums of money, called Danegeld. Like gangsters, the Vikings returned time after time, demanding more money – and land on which they could settle.

INVADING VIKINGS
This painting shows Danish Vikings invading Northumbria. The raiders soon realized how easy it was to attack nearby lands. They began to set up year-round war camps on the coasts. Soon they were occupying large areas of territory and building their own towns.

SAFE AND SOUND
Gold, silver and jewels were locked away in beautiful caskets and chests. This copy of a Viking chest is made of walrus ivory and gilded bronze.

ST CUTHBERT
This picture from the Middle Ages shows St Cuthbert praying in the sea. Cuthbert was one of Lindisfarne's most famous monks. He was made a saint on his death in 687. In 875, when the Danish Vikings attacked the island, the monks fled inland to safety, carrying St Cuthbert's remains.

BUILT FROM THE RUINS
In 793 the Vikings sacked the monastery on Lindisfarne, an island off the coast of northeast England. Afterwards, the religious buildings lay in ruins. The new priory pictured here was built between 1100 and 1200. The stones used to build it were taken from the ruins left by the Vikings. Today, only bare stones remain to remind visitors of the original monastery and its terrible fate.

TREASURE HOARD
This is part of a hoard of about 40kg/90lb of Viking silver. It was found in a chest in Cuerdale, England. The Cuerdale hoard included chopped-up silver ready for melting down, fine brooches and coins from all over the Viking world. Hoards of loot, or wealth, were often buried or hidden away for safety.

The Viking Warrior

THE EARLY VIKING WARRIORS were mostly farmers. They turned their hand to fighting whenever a raiding expedition was organized. Some Vikings became mercenaries – full-time fighters who hired out their services. Later in the Viking Age, kings could conscript, or call up, soldiers to fight a war.

Viking warriors fought hard. To die in battle was their greatest glory – it made sure of their welcome by the gods in Valholl. Leading warriors worked themselves up into a frenzy before battle. They were called *berserkir*, named after their bearskin cloaks.

Much of the fighting took place in skirmishes, ambushes and surprise attacks. In battle, warriors let loose waves of arrows and spears and then charged the enemy lines. Hand-to-hand fighting was brutal. Swords clashed, axes were swung, heavy shields thudded together. There was kicking, biting, bloody wounds and cracked skulls. Viking warriors fought to the bitter end.

SILVER FACE
Bearded and bold – is this the face of a warrior? This lucky charm, made in silver, was worn on a chain around the neck.

SEA WOLVES
The Vikings' enemies wrote of them as if they were packs of wolves, pouring out of the north. They were often cruel and violent, but nobody doubted their extraordinary courage.

BERSERK!
This grim-faced warrior, known as a *berserkir*, is a pawn in a chess set. He is shown in the rage of battle, biting into his shield. This walrus ivory piece was found on Lewis, an island off the coast of Scotland.

MAKE A VIKING HELMET

You will need: tape measure, balloon, petroleum jelly, newspaper, PVA (white) glue, scissors, ruler, card, pair of compasses, water pot, thick brush, fine brush, bronze acrylic paint.

1 First make the main part of the helmet. Use a tape to measure around your head. Blow up a balloon to the same size as your head. Tie the end.

2 Cover half of the balloon in petroleum jelly. Next apply papier mâché. This is made by soaking newspaper strips in water and glue.

3 Allow the papier mâché to dry out and harden. Now burst the balloon. Trim off the ragged edges with scissors until the helmet is neat and round.

THE HORSEMAN

This early stone carving shows a mounted warrior with his sword, shield and hound. While Vikings usually fought battles on foot, they were as skilled at fighting on horseback as they were on board ships. Horses were to play an increasingly important part in later Viking and Norman victories.

SHIELD BY SHIELD

Viking warriors could use their shields to form a defensive wall or as a heavy wedge to break up the enemy lines.

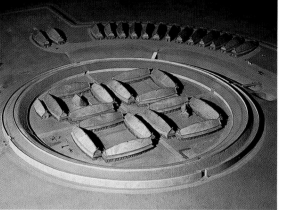

THE FORTRESS

This model shows the earth ramparts of Trelleborg, on the Danish island of Sjælland. It was one of four great forts probably built by Harald Bluetooth in about 980. It would have included barracks and provided shelter for local people in times of warfare.

The wealthier Viking chieftains could afford metal helmets that protected the face from swords and battle axes. A Viking in battle must have been a scary sight.

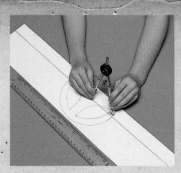

4 Cut a piece of card long enough to fit around the base of the helmet. Use a pair of compasses to draw semicircular patterns on the card, as shown.

5 Cut out the faceguard pattern and glue it onto the rim of the helmet. Cut and glue two long strips of card over the top of the helmet, as shown.

6 When the glue has dried, you can cover the whole helmet in bronze paint. Use a thick brush for the first coat. Then leave the helmet to dry.

7 Use a fine brush to fill in any unpainted areas in the papier mâché to give a neat finish. Make sure the paint is dry before you try the helmet on!

Weapons and Armour

Viking warriors were not like soldiers in an official army. They were not supplied with armour and weapons. They wore their own clothes and brought their own equipment to the battle. Most warriors wore caps of tough leather. Where metal helmets were worn, these were usually conical and they sometimes had a bar to protect the nose. Viking warriors wore their everyday tunics and breeches and cloaks to keep out the cold. A rich jarl might possess a *brynja*, which was a shirt of mail, made up of interlinking rings of iron. The heavy round shield, about 1m/1yd across, was made of wooden planks. It had an iron boss (central knob) and a rim of iron or leather.

On board the longship were spears of various weights, longbows, deadly arrows and long-shafted battle axes. The most prized personal weapon of all was the Viking sword, which often had a beautifully decorated hilt. The blades of the swords were either made by Scandinavian smiths or imported from Germany. To make a sword, a smith would heat up bars of iron, twisting them and beating them into a long blade. Separate cutting edges of tough steel were welded to the blade afterwards.

SPEARHEAD
This Swedish spearhead is made of bronze and its socket is decorated with silver. Broad-bladed spears were designed to be held in the hand. They were used for stabbing. Lighter narrow-bladed spears were used for throwing.

NEW STYLES
This Norwegian knight appears on a tapestry made in about 1180. At the end of the Viking Age, the Normans introduced a long, kite-shaped shield. This was used by the first knights of the Middle Ages, who also wore the mail shirt and a metal helmet with a nasal (nosepiece).

MAKE A SHIELD
You will need: card, scissors, ruler, string, pencil, pair of compasses, gold and red acrylic paints, brush, paper bowl, newspaper, masking tape, PVA (white) glue and brush, foil, paper fasteners, craft (utility) knife, stick, bias binding.

1 Draw a small circle in the middle of the card with the pair of compasses. Then use a length of string tied to a pencil to draw the big circle, as shown above.

2 Cut out the large circle from the card. Then add a design such as the one shown here. Finally paint the shield and leave it to dry.

3 Use a paper party bowl for the shield's central boss, or knob. Scrunch up some newspaper into a flattened ball and tape it to the top of the bowl.

SWORDS AND AXES

These weapons from Jorvik (York) include the remains of two Viking swords with double-edged blades. The iron spearhead would have been fitted onto a light wooden shaft. The Vikings used various axes for hacking the enemy at close range or for throwing from a distance.

WEAPON PARTS

Metal stirrups and weapons have been excavated by archaeologists in many parts of the Viking world. The wood has often rotted away. The iron spearheads and axeheads have survived but not the wooden shafts to which they were fitted.

BY LAND AND SEA

This carved stone from Gotland, Sweden, shows warriors riding and sailing into battle. Vikings used the same weapons at sea as they did on land.

BRONZE HELMET

Goods found in Swedish graves show how wealthy chieftains lived before and during the Viking age. This pre-Viking helmet has a bronze cap with a pattern of warriors, and cheek guards of iron. Most Viking helmets were much less ornate.

Give your shield its own special Viking-style name, such as 'Fist of Thor' or 'Swordbreaker'.

4 Spread glue over the bowl and then cover it with foil. An iron boss would have strengthened the shield and protected the warrior's hand.

5 Glue the boss to the middle of the shield. Secure the boss with paper fasteners punched through the edge and through the card of the shield.

6 Ask an adult to cut a hole with a craft knife in the back of the shield. Glue the stick to the back. Add strips of tape to make it extra secure.

7 Attach the bias binding to the rim of the shield using small dabs of glue (or you could use paper fasteners). Your shield is now ready for battle.

Craftworkers

SNARL OF THE DRAGON
This masterpiece of wood carving and metalwork is a dragon-head post. It is from the Oseberg ship burial in Norway and dates from about 850. Its patterns include monsters known as 'gripping beasts'.

In every Viking home people turned their hand to craft work. The men made and repaired tools and weapons. They carved walrus ivory and wood during long winter evenings. The women made woollen cloth. They washed and combed the wool and then placed it on a long stick called a distaff. The wool was pulled out and spun into yarn on a whirling stick called a spindle. The yarn was woven on a loom, a large upright frame. Blacksmiths' furnaces roared and hammers clanged against anvils as the metal was shaped and re-shaped.

Professional craftworkers worked gold, silver, bronze and pewter – a mixture of tin and lead. They made fine jewellery from amber and from a glassy black stone called jet. Beautiful objects were carved from antlers and ivory from the tusks of walruses. Homes, and later churches, had lovely wood carvings. Patterns included swirling loops and knots, and birds and animals interlaced with writhing snakes and strange monsters.

SWIRLS OF SILVER
This elegant silver brooch was found in Jutland, Denmark. If you look closely, you can see a snake and a beast in the design. The brooch belongs to the late Viking Age.

MAKE A SILVER BRACELET

You will need: tape measure, self-hardening clay, board, scissors, white cord or string, modelling tool, silver acrylic paint, paintbrush, water pot.

1 Measure your wrist with the tape measure to see how big your bracelet should be. Allow room for it to pass over your hand, but not fall off.

2 Roll the clay between the palms of your hand. Make three snakes that are just longer than your wrist measurement. Try to make them of equal thickness.

3 Lay out the three snakes on the board in a fan shape. Cut two lengths of white cord, a bit longer than the snakes, and place them in between.

COLOURS FOR CLOTH

Woollen cloth was dyed in bold shades from leaves, roots, bark and flowers. A wildflower called weld, or dyer's rocket, was used for its yellow dye. The root of the madder gave a red dye. Bright blue came from the leaves of woad plants.

woad   *madder*

THE SMITH AT WORK

This fine wood carving comes from a church in Urnes, Norway. It shows Regin the blacksmith forging a sword on an anvil, for the legendary hero Sigurd. The smith is using bellows to heat up the furnace. The skills of metal working were so important in ancient times that smiths were often seen as magical figures or gods.

TOOLS FROM THE FORGE

Viking blacksmiths used hammers for beating and shaping metal. Tongs were used for handling red-hot iron. Shears were for cutting metal sheets. The blacksmith made everything from nails and knives to farm tools.

Vikings liked to show off their wealth and rank by wearing expensive gold and silver jewellery.

4 While the clay is still soft, plait (braid) the snakes of clay and the two cords together. Ask an adult to help if you are not sure how to make a plait.

5 Trim each end of the plait with a modelling tool. At each end, press the strands firmly together and secure with a small clay snake, as shown above.

6 Carefully curl the bracelet round so that it will fit neatly over your wrist, without joining the ends. Leave it in a safe place to harden and dry.

7 When the bracelet is completely dry, paint it silver. Cover the work surface if necessary. Leave the bracelet to dry again – then try it on!

Art and Music

VIKING SINGING was, by all accounts, a drunken racket that was best avoided! However there must have been skilled Viking musicians, for writers mention fiddles, harps and horns. Musical instruments that have survived include simple flutes made of bone and panpipes made of wood.

In an age when few people could read or write, pictures were often used to tell stories. Pieces of tapestry survive from the Oseberg ship burial. They show a procession of horses and wagons. It is thought that they were woven by noble women. The tradition of making tapestries and embroideries to tell stories and events was continued by the Normans. The Bayeux tapestry was a typical sort of picture story. It celebrated the Norman conquest of England.

The Vikings rarely painted pictures. Art made by the Vikings was mostly carved on wooden panels or stones, or worked in metal. These often show bold, powerful figures, intricate patterns and graceful animals. They demonstrate the Viking artists' love of movement and line.

After the Viking Age, this distinctly Scandinavian style of art disappeared as Europeans brought different styles of art to the area.

TWILIGHT OF THE GODS
This stone carving from the Isle of Man shows the final battle of the gods. Odin, the father of the gods, is shown here armed with a spear and a raven on his shoulder. He is killed by Fenrir, the grey wolf.

ART FROM URNES
At Urnes, in Norway, there is a stave church that has old wood panels. They date from the final years of the Viking Age. This one shows a deer eating Yggdrasil, the tree that holds up the world. Urnes has given its name to the last and most graceful period of Viking art and design.

MAKE A SCARY FACE

You will need: pencil, paper, scissors, self-hardening clay, rolling pin, board, modelling tool, sandpaper, thick brush, acrylic paints, fine brush, water pot.

1 Draw a scary monster face on paper. Copy this one or one from a book, or make up your own. Make your drawing big and bold. Then cut it out.

2 Roll out a large piece of modelling clay into a slab. Use a modelling tool to trim off the edges to look like the uneven shape of a rune stone.

3 Lay your design on top of the clay slab. Use a modelling tool to go over the lines of your drawing, pushing through the paper into the clay.

WOLF BITES GOD

This picture shows Tyr, god of the assemblies and law-makers. His hand is being bitten off by Fenrir, the grey wolf. Fenrir is straining against a magic chain forged by the dwarfs. The chain is made from all sorts of impossible things, such as fish's breath and a mountain's roots. Tyr's name survives in the English word 'Tuesday'.

WHISTLE

This tiny whistle was made from a bird's leg bone. It may have been used to scare birds away from the crops.

WALL HANGING

This boldly designed tapestry shows the gods Odin, Thor and Frey. It comes from a church in Sweden and dates from the 1100s, just after the Viking Age. It is probably similar to the wall hangings woven for royal halls in the earlier Viking times.

4 Go over all the lines in the picture. Make sure the lines show up on the clay below. Remove the paper to see the monster's outline in clay.

5 Leave the clay to dry, turning it over to make sure it is well aired. When it is hard, smooth it down with fine sandpaper, then brush with a paintbrush.

6 Now paint the face as shown, using yellow ochre, black, red and blue. Let each paint dry completely before starting the next. Leave to dry.

Here's a face to scare off evil spirits on a dark night! Faces like this, with interlacing beard and moustache, appeared on stone memorials in the Viking Age.

Ways of Writing

THE VIKINGS developed their own ways of writing. Their alphabet was called the *futhark* after its seven opening letters. All runes (letters) are made up of straight lines and diagonals, because they were designed to be cut into wood, metal or stone. Most runes have survived on stone memorials, which are known as runestones. Historians believe that the Vikings thought the runes, or the runestones themselves, had their own magic. Some Vikings inlaid runes on their sword blades.

It takes a long time to carve runes, so they were only used for short messages. When Christianity came to the Viking lands, the monks needed to write out their holy scriptures. The text was too long to fit onto small bits of wood, so ink and paints were used on a vellum, or calfskin, surface. This was the method that other parts of Europe had been using for some time. There were only 16 runes, and so it had never been a very useful way to communicate. Eventually, the monks began to use the full Roman alphabet instead.

TALES OF EIRIK
The tales of Eirik the Red and his adventures were not written down or carved in runes, in his day. In about 1320 the stories, which had been passed down by word of mouth, were copied out in rather sooty ink on vellum which has darkened with age.

RUNIC ALPHABET
These are the 16 runes used by Danish Vikings. The Norwegian and Swedish version was slightly different.

MAKE YOUR OWN RUNESTONE

You will need: card, pencil, rolling pin, board, self-hardening clay, modelling tool, PVA (white) glue and brush, scissors, red acrylic paint, brush, water pot, soft cloths.

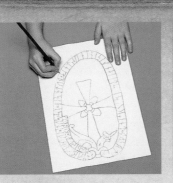

1 Draw the outline of a runestone on card. Draw a line about 5cm/2in in from the edge to make a border. Draw a cross in the middle as shown.

2 Cut out the stone shape. Roll out the clay and lay the card runestone on it. Cut out a neat shape, as above, or leave as a natural-looking runestone, as in picture 5.

3 Cut the border and the cross shape out of the card. Place the card border over the clay and draw round the inside edge of the border, as shown above.

A VIKING HISTORY

Harald Finehair's *Saga* was copied out by hand in 1825, some 435 years after this ruler of Vestfold became the first king of all Norway. The text tells the story of the Viking kings. Although this new tradition of recording events on manuscript became popular, runes were used in Scandinavia well into the Middle Ages.

THE NEW WRITING

As the Viking age drew to a close, skins of sheep, and of calves (vellum) began to be used for writing on. Words could be written down with a quill – the cut end of a feather – and ink. This was easier than carving runes into a stone.

ink

vellum

RUNESTONE

Runestones have been found all over the Viking world. Years of rain and wind have worn them down. They have washed away the bright colours with which they were once painted. Even so, they tell us a great deal about the words and language that were used during the Viking Age.

CELEBRATION

Vikings celebrated the glory of their dead relatives by raising memorial stones in public places. This runestone was put up by Varin for his son Vemod.

Runestones often featured both pictures and writing.

4 Place the card cross shape on the clay. Draw round it with a modelling tool to make an indentation in the clay. Finally, cut runic letters into the clay border.

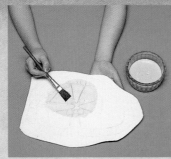

5 Leave the clay to dry until it is completely hard and has gone pale. Then brush watered down PVA glue all over the slab, as shown above.

6 Brush paint over the clay so that it sinks into the indents you have made with the modelling tool. The runes, the border and the cross should stand out.

7 Wipe the clay gently with a damp cloth, to remove all the paint, except in the indents. Leave to dry. Polish with a dry cloth.

Stories and Riddles

AS THE VIKINGS sat around the fire, they told tales about feuds, battles, gods and the histories of their kings. These sagas, or stories, were passed down by word of mouth from one generation to the next. A typical adventure in one saga tells how Harald Hardradi fled from Constantinople. The Empress had ordered chains to be placed across the stretch of water where the ships were anchored. This was to stop the Vikings escaping. The Vikings rowed full tilt towards the chains. At the last moment some of the crew ran to the stern. This made the prow lift out of the water. The boat see-sawed over the chains and sailed away!

Poets called *skålds* travelled from hall to hall. They were expected to sing the praises of their host. If the king or jarl liked the verses, the poet was well rewarded. If he did not like them, the poet's life could be at risk. Poets loved to include riddles in their verses. For example, 'a marvel with eight feet, four eyes and knees higher than its body' was a spider. The audience had to guess what it was.

WRITING IT ALL DOWN
This capital letter has been beautifully decorated. It shows the real life King Harald Finehair cutting the chains of a mythical giant called Dofri. It comes from a book that was made after the Viking Age. Stories that had been told by word of mouth during the Viking years were at last written down as sagas.

THE FINAL BATTLE
This wooden panel tells the story of the last great battle between the gods and the giants. Odin leads the charge against the wolf Fenrir, but is gulped down in the beast's huge jaws.

THE STORY OF SIGURD
Many magical stories were told about an ancient hero named Sigurd. This fine wood carving from the 1100s shows Sigurd slaying a dragon with his great sword. In his other hand he carries a Norman shield.

TOMBSTONE TALES

Ancient Scandinavian myths and legends remained popular well into the Christian period. This is a reconstruction of a tombstone dating from about 1030. Historians believe that it may show a lion in a battle with a serpent. The stone was found in the churchyard of St Paul's Cathedral in England. Archaeologists can imagine how the original tombstone may have looked by the traces of paint left on it. It is thought that the colours on this reconstruction are not very accurate.

THE POET'S REWARD

This massive silver bracelet comes from Falster in Denmark. A skåld might well have received a bracelet like this, or a ring, if the jarl enjoyed the tales that he told in the chieftain's hall.

THE SERPENT OF MIDGARD

In this picture a gigantic monster called the serpent of Midgard thrashes the sea. It is in battle with the hammer-bearing god Thor. The old stories of the Vikings describe the doom of the gods and the destruction of the world. Only when the world is destroyed can a new world be born.

CREATURES OF MYTH

raven

The Vikings were inspired by nature, but they also feared the northern wilderness. The grey wolf howled around their settlements at night. In their minds it became Fenrir, the wolf from hell. When they saw a pair of ravens circling high above them, they thought they must be Hugin and Mugin reporting back to Odin.

wolf

Leisure Pursuits

THE VIKINGS LOVED life. They raced their ships and even tried to run along the oars while the boat was being rowed. Children and adults enjoyed swimming and wrestling, as well as archery, swordplay and weightlifting. Skating and skiing were pastimes as well as means of transport.

Icelanders met up at horse fairs and enjoyed betting on fights between wild ponies. They hunted for pleasure as well as to bring home food. Like their Arab trading partners, the Vikings loved falconry. Wild falcons became a valuable export from the settlements in Greenland. The Vikings used birds of prey to hunt hares and other small animals and birds. Hunting dogs were used as retrievers to collect prey caught by a falcon or hawk.

Festivals were a chance to feast and to forget the northern cold and darkness. The Vikings celebrated midwinter, the coming of summer and the harvest. Evenings by the fire could be taken up with playing dice, or with a board game called *hnefatafl*. In this game, one player had to protect the king from the pieces of the other player. Some boards were beautifully made, while others were very simple. The Vikings also learned how to play the game of chess when they traded in the cities of the Middle East.

GET YOUR SKATES ON

These Viking skates are made of soft leather and were found by archaeologists in York. They have a smooth blade made from an animal bone. Sweden has thousands of lakes that freeze over in winter, and the Vikings were very good skaters. They sometimes used poles to push themselves along.

CHECKMATE!

The pieces in this Viking chess set are made of walrus ivory. They date from the 1100s. The complete chess set was found on the Isle of Lewis, off the west coast of Scotland.

MAKE A HNEFATAFL BOARD

You will need: self-hardening clay, rolling pin, board, modelling tool, ruler, sandpaper, water pot, PVA (white) glue and brush, acrylic paints, paintbrush.

1 Take a large block of red modelling clay. Roll it out flat to cover as large an area as possible without rolling it too thinly. Be sure to roll the clay evenly.

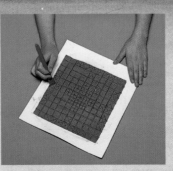

2 Trim the clay to a square, as shown. Score lines on the board, to make 11 x 11 squares. Use your modelling tool to make crosses on the outside and central squares.

3 Sand the board. Give it a coat of watered down glue and leave to dry. Paint the central squares with yellow ochre and the outer squares red. Leave to dry.

DICE

One of these dice is made from bone, the other from walrus ivory. Holes have been drilled to mark the spots on the dice. The Vikings loved board games. Long ago, these dice would have been rattling on a bench or table in the chieftain's hall.

IRISH GAMES

This games board comes from Ballinderry in Ireland. It may have been used for playing hnefatafl. The Vikings loved gambling and all kinds of games.

PRIZED FALCONS

The Bayeux tapestry shows a falconer wading on board King Harold's ship. Falconry was one of the most popular forms of hunting in Europe and would have been very familiar to Vikings and Normans.

Hnefatafl was the Vikings' best-loved board game for winter evenings. The pieces would have been made of chalk and amber.

4 Make nine clay playing pieces, of which one 'king' is bigger. When dry, paint the king and three other pieces black and paint five pieces white.

5 Place the black king in the middle, surrounded by the other black pieces. Place the white pieces on the red patterned squares at the edges.

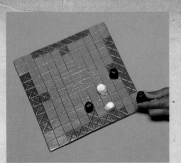

6 Players take turns to move the pieces across the board. Hnefatafl is played rather like of chess or draughts (checkers). The aim is to take the king.

7 Make up some rules for the game. Decide which way the pieces can move and by how many squares. Do not forget to decide how the game is won!

Viking Burials

THE END of a Viking's life was marked with a funeral. Kings, queens and other rich Vikings were often buried with treasures to use in the next world. Sometimes slaves were killed and buried with them. Less wealthy Vikings might travel to the next world with their sword or the tools of their trade. The kings and queens of Denmark were buried in stone chambers inside great mounds at Jelling. Large runestones were raised as memorials to the dead. Relatives carved inscriptions on these stones, telling of the loved ones they had lost. In parts of the British Isles, Viking settlers took on the local custom of carving gravestones.

Seafaring was very important to the Viking way of life. As a result, the custom grew up of burying important people in splendid ships. People believed that the dead would use these ships to sail to the next world. Burial ships were usually buried under mounds, or sometimes they were set on fire at sea in a great, final blaze.

FROM THE GRAVE
This fine bucket was found in a woman's grave at Birka, in Sweden. It is made of wood covered with bronze. It was probably made in the British Isles about 1,100 years ago.

SHIP SHAPES
These stones were erected in the shape of a longship. They mark a Viking grave in Gotland, Sweden. Burial stones such as these are quite common throughout Scandinavia. These ship burial sites symbolize the idea of death as a voyage into the unknown.

Up-Helly-Aa

At the end of January a festival is held in the Shetland Isles. A model Viking ship is set ablaze with flaming torches. It marks the end of the midwinter festival, Up-Helly-Aa. No one really knows the origin of this festival but one story by an Arab chronicler talks of a similar event, the burning of a Viking burial boat on the river Volga.

The Gokstad Ship

This royal ship was excavated from a burial mound at Gokstad in 1880. It was rebuilt and can be seen today in the Viking Ship Museum at Bygdøy, Norway.

Goods
from Graves

This beautiful silver cup was found in a royal burial mound at Jelling, in Denmark. It was probably buried with King Gorm, father of Harald Bluetooth, sometime around the year 958. Although it is likely that King Gorm's body was buried with many other items, few remained when the tomb was excavated. It is likely that the chamber was entered hundreds of years ago and the goods mysteriously removed in an orderly fashion.

Glossary

A

anvil An iron block used for shaping metal in a smithy.
archaeologist Someone who makes a scientific study of ancient remains and ruins.

B

brazier

berserkir Viking warriors who worked themselves up into a frenzy of rage before battle. They were named after their bearskin cloaks or shirts.
brazier A metal stand for holding burning coals.
brynja A warrior's tunic made of iron rings, or mail.
burial ship Vikings were sometimes buried or cremated in finely decorated wooden ships.
byre A cowshed.

C

caulk To seal the planks of a ship with tar or other material, so that it stays watertight.
chalice The ceremonial cup, often of silver or gold, used by Christian priests to hold wine.
colonize To settle in a foreign land or colony.

D

Danegeld Money paid to Vikings by English or French rulers to prevent their being attacked.
die A tool for punching a design into metal.
distaff A long stick used to hold wool while it is being spun.

drinking horn The hollow horn of a cow, often decorated with silver and used as a drinking cup.

F

faering A small rowing boat used for fishing or coastal journeys.
falconry Using birds of prey to hunt other birds or animals.
feud A long-standing quarrel, especially between two families.
fjord A deep sea inlet formed long ago by the action of ice. The Norwegian coast has many fjords.
fort A fortified military position. Viking forts had a strict geometrical

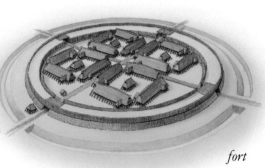
fort

layout. Each one lay within a high circular rampart of earth and turf.

G

graffiti Words or pictures that have been scratched or written on to a wall, statue or other object.
gripping beast A design used by Viking craft workers, in which animals or monsters are shown locked in combat.

H

Hedeby An important Danish Viking town (now in Germany).
hnefatafl A popular boardgame played in Viking times.

J

jarl A Viking chieftain. The word is linked to the English 'earl'.

K

karl A free-born Viking man, able to own land, trade and fight.
keel The long beam that supports the frame of a wooden ship, running along the base of the hull.
knarr A sturdy trading ship, designed to carry cargo.

L

Law Speaker The person who read out the laws passed by the assembly of free Vikings.
longhouse The chief building of a Viking farmstead, including a great hall.
longship A long, sea-going vessel used by the Vikings for warfare or exploration.
loom A wooden frame used for weaving cloth.

M

mercenary A soldier who hires out his services to an army for money.
midden A rubbish tip or dunghill.

longship

Midgard Vikings believed that Midgard was the human world.

myth Any ancient story about gods, magic and imaginary places.

N

nasal A metal bar fitted to a helmet to protect the nose.

Norman A descendant of the Vikings who settled in northern France.

O

Odin The most powerful and mysterious god. He was the god of war, magic and poetry.

P

pagan Pre-Christian, worshipping the old gods of nature and the countryside.

pewter An alloy, or mixture of metals, made from tin and lead.

picture stone A memorial stone carved with pictures.

prow The front end of a ship. Longship prows were often carved with dragon heads.

Q

quern stone A stone used for grinding flour.

R

rampart A defensive mound of earth.

republic A land that is not ruled by a king, queen or emperor.

rigging The ropes used to support a ship's mast and sails.

rune One of the symbols made up of lines, used as letters of the alphabet by the peoples of ancient Germany and Scandinavia.

runestone A memorial stone

picture stone

carved with runes.

Rus The name given to Swedish traders who settled in eastern Europe.

S

saga A family history or heroic tale told by storytellers in old Scandinavia or Iceland.

skáld A Viking poet, storyteller and inventor of riddles.

spindle A whirling tool used to make fibre, such as wool, into yarn for weaving.

stave A plank made from splitting a tree trunk.

stern The rear end of a ship.

strake One of the long, overlapping planks running along the side of a longship.

T

tapestry A cloth with a picture or design woven by hand on its threads.

Thing An assembly of free men, which passed laws in Viking lands. The Icelandic assembly was called the Althing.

Thor The fierce, red-bearded god of thunder.

thrall A slave.

treasure hoard A stash of treasure buried for safe-keeping.

V

Valholl or Valhalla The great hall of the gods, where brave Viking warriors were welcomed after death.

valkyrie In Viking myths, the valkyrie was one of Odin's female attendants, who welcomed heroes to Valholl. She was sometimes shown as an old hag who hovered over battlefields like a vulture.

Viking One of the Scandinavian peoples who lived by sea raiding in the early Middle Ages.

treasure hoard

Vinland The name given by the Vikings to part of the North American coast (Newfoundland).

W

wagons Carved wooden carts, sometimes used in burials as coffins.

wattle and daub A method of making walls or fences by interlacing sticks and covering them with clay.

weather vane A light metal plate used to show the direction of the wind.

valkyrie

Index